AMBIVALID,

OR
"STAGGERING TOWARDS VIRTUE"

AND

BACK IN THE HOLY BRONX

BY
J.R. MCCARTHY

First Serious Ink Press Edition published June, 2007

Copyright 2007 by Serious Ink Press

All rights reserved. Published in the United States by Serious Ink Press, a division of Artists I Love, LP. No part of this publication may be reproduced or transmitted in any form or by any means, electronic or mechanical, including photocopy, recording, or any other information storage and retrieval system, without prior permission in writing from the publisher.

Printed in U.S.A.

Serious Ink Press ISBN- 10: 0-9796985-0-2
Serious Ink Press ISBN- 13: 978-0-9796985-0-7

The text of this book is composed in Baskerville with the dispaly set in Copperplate

Book design by S. Kaldon

www.seriousinkpress.com
www.artistsilove.com

2 3 4 5 6 7 8 9 0

I am delighted and honored to benefit from the support and expertise of two of my oldest and dearest friends. I thank my editor, Steve Kaldon, for his patience and sensitivity. I thank my publisher, Tom McGeady, whose beautiful brainchild, Artists I Love.com is currently providing many of us with the best possible platform from which to further our hopes.

Nothing works or matters without the love and appraising gazes of my wife, Tricia. I love you, La Sposa Bella.

−J.R. McCarthy

AMBIVALID,

OR

"STAGGERING TOWARDS VIRTUE"

AND

BACK IN THE HOLY BRONX

AMBIVALID 1

BACK IN THE HOLY BRONX 39

ABOUT J.R. MCCARTHY 46

Ambivalid,
or
"Staggering Towards Virtue"

I.

"Money"

There was a residential community called "Money"
and in its red brick buildings
there lived thousands of people.

The mapmakers divided it into four quadrants,
and they gave the quadrants most impressive names:

The quadrant to the North was "Security".
The quadrant to the South was "Influence".
The quadrant to the West was "Expedience".
The quadrant to the East was "Luxury".

Every map is a guide for the prospective citizen, who agrees to
become a resident before he passes a single night,
and may not care where the vacancies happen to be.

But the residents in their beds –
suddenly awakened in the middle of the night –
can tell you exactly where they live.
And they can tell you exactly why
their part of town is the least desirable.

II.

Haiku Invoked Against Vandalism

As far as I know,
you will be all right if they
only break your heart.

It won't seem so at
the time, or any time soon,
because you don't yet

Know what you must learn:
people who break things are mad
that they can't have them.

They don't have the strength
or the courage to steal them,
and they certainly

cannot come by them
honestly. So there you are,
a vandal is born.

III.

HAIKU INVOKED AGAINST IDLE HANDS

Let me never be
separated from the things
that keep me busy.

Don't let me languish
in a place where the minutes
need to be counted.

Having said this much,
and until those sister hags,
Duty and Routine,

have blocked every path
to the colorful contours
of my human mind,

lay the blame before
my shoeless feet whenever
my hands are idle.

6 Ambivalid

IV.

"SEX"

There was a residential community called "Sex",
and in its red brick buildings,
there lived thousands of people.

The mapmakers divided it into four quadrants,
and they gave the quadrants most impressive names:

The quadrant to the North was "Procreation"
The quadrant to the South was "Pleasure"
The quadrant to the West was "Intimacy"
The quadrant to the East was "Completion"

A map is a guide for the stranger,
who thus becomes aware of the lay of the land
long before his motives are known,
and regardless of what his motives may be.

But the residents in their beds –
suddenly awakened in the middle of the night –
were unable to say which quadrant they were in
unless they had someone to ask,
or they could begin to remember.

V.

Haiku Invoked Against Casual Sex

Before this night ends
I will remove my clothing
before a stranger –

One I don't yet know
will savor my pastiness
and endure my girth;

until I leap up,
consumed by great self-loathing,
to get her a coke.

Dear friends and heroes
who dwell with my grandparents
in a paradise

I shall never see:
if there be blocks where you are,
please walk around them

for the next cycle
of my long adolescence.
I can't bear the thought

that somewhere up there,
among the sated spirits,
you are giggling.

VI.

Haiku Invoked Against Excess

I will share a dream
That I would have been happy
never to have had:

I die in this dream,
and wherever I wound up,
they tell me, "Listen!

Scarf, smoke, or guzzle
whatever your heart desires,
but your three youngest

nieces and nephews
have to match your excesses
poison for poison."

Now Emily hates
cigars, Anna flees from the
first whiff of whiskey,

and Edward just prays
that sooner or later they'll
run out of doughnuts.

VII.

"THE CYNIC"

Let us praise the cynic,
for the ways of the cynic are smart
and the precepts of the cynic
are easy to learn,
and even easier to remember.

The pronouncements of the cynic are clever,
and at least as humorous as a joke
at the expense of a dead celebrity.

Let us praise the cynic,
and perhaps he will prosper
enough to begin to appreciate
the value of ulterior motives –

or perhaps he will just go away.

Day after day,
the cynic eats a sumptuous lunch
in glorious solitude –
but he is stone,
and stone he will remain.

Only statues and cynics
are really alone in the crowd.

VIII.

THE BALLAD OF COVET MUCH

We desired what we spoiled.
We admired what we ruined.
We have foiled our aspirations
by destroying what we want.
We obsess about the peace you
undermined because you showed us
all your pretty little somethings
long before you got to know us.

Won't you join us? We will tarry
for a while in the dreamland
where we first beheld the things
we were convinced would make us happy.
Won't you join us? We will tally
all the things we have devalued
with the tinge of our resentment
as we worked to make them no ones'.

On the downside, we beheld the thing
we needed to complete us
in your ignorant possession,
and resolved to make it worthless.
On the upside, you were with us
from the shores of disappointment
to the depths of desolation
long before you got to know us.

Won't you join us? We will tarry
for a while in the dreamland
where we first beheld the things
we were convinced would make us happy.
Won't you join us? We will tally
all the things we have devalued
with the tinge of our resentment
as we worked to make them no ones'.

Had we stared through our first blindness
at the parents of our cellmates,
we'd despise the breasts and knuckles
that were proffered to our newness.
We would hardly keep composure
In the face of all good fortune
And our plots may have unraveled
Long before you got to know us.

Won't you join us? We will tarry
for a while in the dreamland
where we first beheld the things
we were convinced would make us happy.
Won't you join us? We will tally
all the things we have devalued
with the tinge of our resentment
as we worked to make them no ones'.

IX.

SELFISHBASTARDAVARICIOUS-
EXPIALIDOCIOUS

I could grab with both my hands
if only I could drop this
pretence that it's nice to share
with strangers and with nitwits
who let old folks cut the line, and
like the size of peach pits:
What's the point of sowing
what you won't be here to reap?

I could grab with both my hands
if only I was free of
spouse and offspring, family, friends
and any dull acquaintance
With a cause or hair-brained scheme,
and means to my attention:
What's the point of sowing
what you won't be here to reap?

I could grab with both my hands
if this capricious ocean
had the salt to buoy me
and all of my possessions:
sink with all my pretty things
or start all over empty –
What's the point of sowing
what you won't be here to reap?

More than one house,
more than two cars
more than three deposit
boxes in the local bank –
and four more in the closet:
quarters from all fifty states and
several wooden nickels;
more crap from the Franklin Mint
my heirs can throw away.
things that would have been thrown out
and things that would have spoiled
things that should have been locked up
if they were so important
things I only recently
remembered I possess,
they were rediscovered
as I searched for something else.

I could grab with both my hands
if I could bend my fingers:
thus betrayed by ancient joints,
my posture says surrender.
Younger robber barons raze
my fields, and I don't blame them –
What's the sense of sowing
what you won't be here to reap?

X.

"The Scoundrel"

Let us praise the Scoundrel:
for the ways of the Scoundrel are
predictable in retrospect.

The precepts of the Scoundrel
are precedents he will help you to uncover.

The pronouncements of the Scoundrel
will help you to be more articulate
the next time you talk to yourself,
or attempt to charm a bone from a dog.

 Let us continue to praise the Scoundrel
with our accustomed adjectives of indignation:

He cannot even imagine
that we mean what we say about him.

Night after night,
the Scoundrel sleeps like a baby –
but he is in Hell,
and in Hell he will remain:

Only cadavers and scoundrels
are unmolested by mixed emotions.

XI.

LECHERY IS THE BEST POLICY

Here is the whole of my soul against
two dimensions of your celebrated flesh.
Here is the odd and even of my messy
solitaire against the figment of you.

It's better to be strangers than to make believe
I appreciate the clamor of your cacophony,
but the false dream won't desert me.

It's better to be strangers than to become creepy,
and vindicate the yammering of your detractors.
but the false dream won't desert me.

Here is the whole of my day against
yet another chance to watch you walk.
Here is the back and forth of
my cage- pace until your screen door slams.

It is better to be invisible than to
have to sweat through another exposure
to your tantalizing listlessness,

It is better to be invisible than to
dance by the light of the attic
while you disappoint another cretin.

You show my tree-like friends
that the tyranny of belts and buttons
has branded your unblemished belly,
and the false dream won't desert me.

Two identical daisies brush against
the faded number on the front of your jersey –
one if by land; two if by sea –
and the false dream won't desert me.

16 Ambivalid

You invite me to call you back
so you can snub me a second time,
but the false dream won't desert me.

I smuggled these pictures past the police,
and you're not even smiling,
but the false dream won't desert me.

I shucked off my blubber,
and baked you a tin of sonnets:
you look at me as if you don't know me,
but the false dream won't desert me.

I can't believe my haggard, humbled
heart still pumps bothered blood
but the false dream won't desert me.

XII.

Gluttonous Maximus

Gluttonous Maximus belched like a pro,
and growled at his thin retinue,
"I swear by my chins, I shall broil the next
bag of bones who suggests that I chew.
The teeth I have left are as rotten as death,
and my gums are all swollen and blue.
It just goes to show you that one out of
four of you dentists do not have a clue."

I ate without chewing, I ate without tasting,
I ate without breathing. I ate without dressing
and needless to say, I ate without checking
to see if the others were left with a crumb.
I ate without tools and I ate without plates,
and I ate without sitting my ass on a chair,
and now that it's over I finally see that
I ate without noticing you standing there.

Gluttonous Maximus pissed like a racehorse,
and shot-gunned a flagon of mead.
His urine bounced off of the wall of the alley
and spread through his old gabardine.
Inasmuch as his subjects had found their way home
several hours before, he decided
To wheedle his car keys away from the barkeep:
designating himself as the driver.

I drank without friends and I drank without reason
and if memory serves me, in all of four seasons.
I drank in the park when the weather was freezing.
I drank in the bar when the weather was fair.
It was dark when I started, and light when I stopped
at the local Greek diner to gorge on éclairs –
And if I'd had the courage to keep up the pace,
I'd be drinking today at the end of this race.

18 Ambivalid

Gluttonous Maximus watched his own wake
on a black and white T.V. in Hell.
Three hours in he gave up on his widow:
she'd not come to bid him farewell.
His coffin resembled a portable cooler.
His mourners had wondered away
as soon as the funeral parlor confirmed
that there would not be any buffet.

I lived at a pace and I lived with a will that
left little room for aerobics or sleep.
I lived for a break and I lived for a taste and
my life ended slowly, so nobody weeps

Nobody weeps
because nobody's left
when Gluttonous Maximus
comes to his end,

Nobody weeps,
and nobody learns
because Gluttonous Maximus
ate all his friends.

XIII.

"POWER"

There was a residential community called "Power",
and in its red brick buildings
there lived thousands of people.

The mapmakers divided it into four quadrants,
and they gave the quadrants most impressive names:

The quadrant to the North was called "Control";
The quadrant to the South was called "Advantage";
The quadrant to the West was called "Freedom"
The quadrant to the East was called " Prominence".

A map is a visitor's chance to learn about where things are,
for only then may he avoid the things he does not want.

But the residents, avoiding their beds,
and peeking out their windows all night
like nothing less than visitors,
and like nothing more than new neighbors.

XIV.

"Haiku Invoked Against Self-Importance"

A nun who was once
my teacher cornered me at
Sterling Optical,

She wanted to know
what I had made of my gifts.
I told her, Sorry,

Sister. Love to bring
you up to speed, but I must
go to Olympus

and round up my wife
as per my arrangement with
her heartsick mother.

Then, of course, it's back
to Hades, and terrible
judgment of the dead.

A little white lie:
I'm really resuming my throne
Among the blind men.

XV.

"Haiku Invoked Against Self-Pity"

How flattered I am
to hear that I was replaced
by a committee!

Now, folks approach me
everywhere I go, saying
how much they miss me;

how they dearly wish
I was back "behind the wheel",
for I understood

what they required;
how sick they are of telling
service providers

how to do their jobs.
They are happy to tell me
their horror stories

of the committee's
vain and strident ignorance.
"All is lost!" they cry.

"Thank you for sharing,"
sez I , "but I must get back
to the chain gang now."

XVI.

"The Taskmaster"

Let us now praise the Taskmaster,
For the ways of the Taskmaster are exacting,
And as unambiguous as they are
Uninspiring.

The precepts of the Taskmaster
are the same as they were
when the first hunting party was formed,

and the pronouncements of the Taskmaster
will always be arranged in convenient call and response:

You can listen to them later
while you and your friends are in hiding.

Night after night,
the Taskmaster goes to bed extra-early:
but he can't sleep
and sleep he never shall:

Only scouts and taskmasters
know the Legions of the Messy Inevitable
by the tramp of their muddy boots.

XVII.

"VANITY FADES"

I was born with a wrench I turned into a hammer,
and I hammered away at the bolts and the nuts.
As I squeezed myself into the ranks of the poets
on the strength of a tiny collection of puns,
I knew in my heart that when I became famous,
I would grind on the shoulders of one in the dust.
and the statue of me may be bleached by the sun,
but it stands on a bland congregation of slugs.

I was born with a wrench I turned into a hammer
and I hammered away at the nuts and the screws.
I beat down the long-dead corpse of the villain
and posed like St. George; put one big borrowed boot
on the motionless throat – Now! if that's not an image
to pause and to save, just stop talking, and shoot.
And the statue of me may be deep in the park,
but I see it just fine from this lonely old room.

I was born with a wrench I turned into a hammer,
and I hammered away at the screws and the bolts.
For Vanity's sake, I have flooded the kitchen.
For Vanity's sake, I set fire to the rug.
But my flesh is as dry as the reams of blank paper,
and the brew that once boiled in my veins is now cold.
And the statue of me deserves each bit of bird shit
that hangs from its sensitive nose.

XVIII.

"Two Sonnets for My Righteous Wrath"

I

You are the only lover I require.
I swear that I will curse all those who try
with logic or their god-damned love to ply
my will to will the quenching of this fire.
You are the only lover I require
and to your brimstone fortress I will fly
when fops and fatheads make bold to imply
that you are false, and let yourself be squired
by other suitors. Don't you know I'd flay
the blushing flesh right off your living frame
if you should ever dare or make to stray?
So have I savaged many I could name
whose crime was to suggest I but delay
before I fed more fuel into your flame.

II

I often culled the heat of my devout
and raging love into a killing beam
that burned until it thoroughly unseamed
your enemies. But you, you ageless lout
set me aflame only to throw me out
when you were done! I raged, and did not dream
your potion was a poison 'til the stream
that fueled my foolish passion was about
to kill my heart. And if my heart still pounds,
'tis but to curse your name, and rue the hour
that forms as yet unborn will dance around
in grateful rains, their heartfelt hopes to flower,
while my poor heart, wedged deep in barren ground,
is too far gone for any saving power.

XIX.

"SKILL"

There was a residential community called "Skill",
and in its red brick buildings,
there lived thousands of people.

The mapmakers divided it into four quadrants,
and they gave the quadrants most impressive names:

The quadrant to the North was called, "Accomplishment"
The quadrant to the South was called "Identity";
The quadrant to the West was called, "Direction";
The quadrant to the East was called, "Therapy".

A Map will help you discover the things for which you search,
and it also may reveal to you some things you might like to see.

If the residents have not yet taken to their beds
they will show you certain wonders when you visit,

but if you arrive after they have fallen asleep,
you will not be able to wake them.

XX.

"Haiku Invoked Against Obliviousness"

"Regular Pizza
and an honest cup of Joe
would be nice right now. "

my Dear Old Dad says,
chuckling softly to himself,
"And the people on

those cell phones look like
they're talking to Mr. Spock,
or maybe themselves . . ."

Now am I willing
to believe he's really back.
Now I understand

the true purpose of
his long awaited return.
As the two of us

visit Manhattan,
walking Second Avenue
down to Houston Street,

I notice changes
in everything around me
for the first time since

he died. It's as if
I just stopped noticing life
once he disappeared.

XXI.

"The Procrastinator"

Let us now praise the procrastinator
– and someone please tell him
the nice things we said
when he finally arrives –

for the ways of the procrastinator are flexible
and the precepts of the procrastinator
will envelop the wisdom of all
if ever they may be written.

The pronouncements of the procrastinator
are spontaneous,
and need only be memorized
by those who have rejected them.

Time after time,
the Procrastinator pledges allegiance
To the future,
but his "now" is the same as his "then"
and his "then" will never come –

Only satellites and procrastinators
Are undeterred by the latest developments.

XXII.

"Acedia Beat"

Now freedom comes not with a turn of a key,
but with a rattle of the cage. Now I prove with my soft shoulder
that the door has always been unbolted. Now I push,
and the bones of many chances become dust upon my path.

Now the sun bathes me as if I have always been here.

Now is the time when something may lead to something else.
Now do I want now, and welcome joy. Now do I cast out soon,
and now does now become forever, and forever more.

Now I begin as if it was still the beginning.

Now I begin again and again and again as required.

Now do I see I was harried by nothing but phantoms.
Now do I see I was exhausted by nothing but sorrow.

Now do I know:
It is better to be wicked than it is to be ungrateful.
It is better to be wrong than it is to be indifferent.
It is better to be misdirected than it is to be unmoving.

Now that it is possible to be, may it be possible to build.
Now that it is possible to engage, may it be possible to extend.
Now that it is possible to surmount, may it be possible to surround.
Now that it is possible, may it be now.

Long live the now in the several beginnings.
Long live the now in the celebration of the former flesh.
Long live the now in the truce that becomes an embrace.

Long live the now
as it moves beyond speech to strength.
Long live the now
as I keep a thousand promises to one love.
Long live the now
as I keep one promise to a thousand loves.
Long live the now
as the flame fires forever.

Long live the now.
Long live the now.
Long live the now.

XXIII.

Epilogue

"Dignity"
The mark of worthiness
is occasional feelings of unworthiness.
The mark of adequacy
is occasional feelings of inadequacy.

Even at this safe remove,
I have moments of longing
for the conviction of ignorance.
Even at this steady pace,
I am sometimes tempted to flirt
with the force of my arrogance.

Do not be anxious
about your anxious moments.
Cultivate the same sense of modesty
about the substance of your turmoil
that you have imposed upon
your real and radiant beauty:
This is the practice of Dignity.

"Patience"
You will know what you know when you know it,
but your ability to pass on your willingness
will never exceed your willingness to return to your ignorance.

Certainty will certainly be yours to extend,
and will forever be others' to refuse.

Others may be enlightened, but you will never instruct them.
Others may be inspired, but you will never persuade them.

There is no teaching: there is only
the demonstration that it is possible
to learn how to learn.

Encourage the needful to avail themselves
of the power of repetition.
Offer yourself as a silent example
of the gentle influence of effort.
This is the practice of Patience.

"Gratitude"
When the soul no longer hates itself
because it needed a little assistance;
when the soul is no longer oppressed
by the ledgers of credit or debt;
when the soul is invigorated
by the drive to give back and go forward;
freedom is finally possible.

The indecipherable Writ
of Everything I Owe to Everyone
will be buried in one of the few places
where dust is still allowed to gather,

Resentment and regret
will cease to blind you
to all the good you can do –

Your damp face will incline
to receive the kiss of kindness,
and you'll go find someone to help.

This is the beginning
of the practice of Gratitude.

"Compassion"
The smallest sorrow long endured
will break the strongest back,
but four slender shoulders
could have buoyed the grief of Job.

Guilt and shame may warrant the burden of sorrow,
but not even justice may call that sorrow good.

Your sorrow may have been imposed upon you
or it may be the fruit of your own viciousness,
but carry it you must, and carry it you shall.

Accept for once and for all
that the sorrow of one diminishes each.

If you cannot join the work of rehabilitation,
you must not scuttle it with your scorn.

Live, and let the convicted live.
Keep your big fat thumb off the scale.
This is the bare beginning
of the practice of Compassion.

XXIV.

Addendum: "Epistemology 101"

A:
In a universe so little more than open space,
you would think that every miracle was obvious.
It would figure that each gracious act was plain to see
and as subject to concealment as a galaxy.
But let all of us remember that duality
is the nature of things subject to credulity.
Thus, reality itself we rightly separate
into opposites called "emptiness" and "aggregate"

Where the universe is empty, it's completely so
and you find yourself nowhere no matter where you go:
a depressing thing for all of us to contemplate
while we reside within the crowded Aggregate,
where everything that takes up space has been consigned
but tight within its own volume has been confined.
When from each crowded place we seek to understand
what can be learned or sensed about the master plan
we see that while the emptiness is wide and vast,
the aggregate is infinitely various.

Considering that emptiness is thus revealed
to be no more than digesting this one idea
of vast and simple nothingness, and nothing more
it seems to have no purpose save to underscore
that what seems like a mess of things to you and me.
are really entities of poignant rarity:
In a universe that's mostly made of empty space
anywhere that's anywhere's a sacred place.

34 Ambivalid

Alack, alas! This crowd , including you and I,
and millions of our ancestors, and theirs besides
reside within this ghetto of the aggregate
and see ourselves as atoms in a cluttered pit
of pretty much the same when in reality,
we're each of us the soul of singularity.
We're each of us the soul of singularity
without a single instance of redundancy.
it isn't just some pose of eccentricity
that separates the Crowd of You from Holy Me.

And, so much more important, from my point of view,
is the simple singularity of Holy You.
I can't believe that all my precious reverie
was trapped in the forsaken rut of "only me."
for now I see that what I saw as retinue
is really mile after mile of Holy You.
And what I see of you I truly need to see
before I can resemble what is Wholly Me.

B:
Between the tongs of "not a thing" and "everything"
we thus extract the pearl of singularity.
We wax ironic, and observe that preciousness
can only be perceived among the various.
The wisest man I ever knew once said to me,
"All priceless things are worthless, son" Now, can it be
that a wise man uttered something that was sensible,
practical and utterly defensible?

The final mark of worth within this worthy world
resides within the aforementioned single pearl
precisely since it's there for everyone to grasp
as many times as grateful grasping hands can clasp
And just as soon as everyone has gotten one
a million more are glistening in the morning sun:
each in the gracious state of being singular,
but only in this sense the least bit similar.

We live within the ghetto of the aggregate
where wealth became the wherewithal to isolate
what we desire with the undesirable
idea that what is generally attainable
is not for me – that something there for each of us
is hardly worth the strength it takes to pick it up.
We live within the ghetto of the aggregate
where comfort must be ransomed from the wretched state
of emptiness that grinds the things that it consumes
until they're only fit for dust on Pharaoh's Tomb.

But we'll escape this slum of misbegotten rules,
of poison maxims leaking out of toxic schools
of Not One Blessed Thought that ever earned the right
to be repeated once the darkness turned to light.
We'll escape the Ghetto of the Aggregate
and pound the dust of pharaoh from our birthday suits
With open palms we've fashioned out of unclenched fists
we'd wrapped around those trinkets we've learned to resist.

When we are all thus liberated, history
will give us leave to call a new consistory
and contemplate exhilarating evidence
that what was once a ghetto is now tenantless.
And inasmuch as there's no ghetto anymore,
The Earth will be one neighborhood from crust to core.
And what was once an orb will be a roundabout
and none shall live within whom we can do without
We'll be the tribe of Holy You and Holy Me,
and worthy of the God of Relativity.

C:
Long have I longed for single-minded certainty
and cherish I the thought that my posterity
will one day learn of my attempt to make the mass
of people step up out of this replete morass
of various benighted ideologies
and try to dig the God of Relativity.
Am I insane or out of line if I should say
that hierarchy has already had its day
and now must be delivered to the crackling fire
that currently all bigotry and fear devours:?

Am I an ingrate if I tell my friends and folks
that many of their verities are tired jokes,
and will disintegrate at dawn's first pearly light
when we passed through this excruciating night?
And will you move to put me in my painful place
if I proclaim that God will let us see his face
(or her face, or their faces, as the case may be.)
when we look up from dusty floors and palmistry
and Love God as the God of Relativity?

Our ancestors believed in imbecility,
and did not know the God of Relativity.
Their ancestors were blind to their periphery
and could not know the God of Relativity.
My colleagues so adhere to the majority
that they can't find the God of Relativity
My neighbors gloat that they are the minority
and this excludes the God of Relativity.

I make no challenge to the purely human urge
of human hearts to parse the very Demiurge
into a thing that they can finally understand
and undertake to inculcate, but would you stand
up with me now, and now forever we'll decry
the tendency of human beings to vilify
and bury in what ends up being Holy Ground
the one or ones who cannot wrap themselves around
the credo of the month, or the millennium?
Now may I bring an end to this symposium....

But first I'll say what all of us should well recall
"Holier Than Thou" preceded Satan's fall.
None Holier Than Thou: the only verity
and etched here by the God of Relativity.
Holy You and Holy Me – and wholly, we
are precious to the God of Relativity.
HOLY IS AS HOLY DOES: Philosophy
and Nature of the God of Relativity.

Back in the Holy Bronx

I

I am back in the Holy Bronx,
where my father and his father
and his father rest in what peace there is
I'm back in the Holy Bronx,
carrying on in the name of shadows
as they gather into legends. Noble Antecedents!
I am driving by your graves and wondering
if you really listen to the things we say,
and really watch all the things we do.
Am I thinking of you because you're thinking of me?
Do you signify to me that Heaven
is no better than the Holy Bronx, so
I should stay put, and Mother should, too?

Holy Bronx, you too have been ensnared by
the encroaching anonymity of American cities.
Your German delis implode into snapshot temples,
and your beauty schools become vegetable maxi-marts.
Your dimly lit bodegas sold beer to minors,
but who sells minors to beer more quickly than
the Videodrome and the Smoketeria?
Holy Bronx, I swear you
kept your children out of your saloons:
they shivered over cheap wine in the pits
of your arcane masonry until they came of age.
Holy Bronx, I swear you
sent your children off to worship on the many
Sabbaths, but they sneaked off to the park
to share kaiser rolls, and that's not your fault.

Back in the Holy Bronx

Holy Bronx, you have more
Ravishing Latin Girls than San Cipriano
could raise from the sea foam on Orchard Beach.
Holy Bronx, you have more
Glorious Irish Girls in County Woodlawn
than the White Brothers can hypnotize
with their famous blue eyes.
Holy Bronx, you have more
Magnificent Italian Girls in the Curio shops
of Arthur Avenue than the world may know.
Holy Bronx, you have even more
Fascinating Black Girls than you know yourself:
why are your poets too proud to
shape sweet lyrics for their bangled ears?

Holy Bronx, you rock with reckless wisdom.
Holy Bronx , you damn cowards to invisibility.
Holy Bronx, you breathe history and
your rooftops are littered with homers.
Lilt of the Holy Bronx upon my tongue;
Bounce of the Holy Bronx in my walk;
All the way up Webster Avenue from now
until Yonkers, amen.

II

I am back in the Holy Bronx,
driving badly in one of the many
family cars I have squired to Death.
I am back in the Holy Bronx,
crawling from Jerome to Gunhill
because my lady dreads I 95, or
double-parking on East Tremont because
people in Nyack are jonesing for cannolis.
Lou Gehrig and Sal Mineo,
Virginia Clemm and Leatrice Joy

Billie Holiday and Big Pun, would you give
up the Elysian Fields to get a glimpse
of dinosaurs lumbering up Fordham Road,
or spaceships docking at Ferry Point Park?

Holy Bronx, you are giggling like a school girl
at the thugs of the Third Millennium,
tripping on their clown pants, cramming
baseball caps on top of bandannas on top
of 'do-rags. What happened to satin-backed,
singing marauders, to gangs with soul,
and soul with shape and shape showing
up with her friends just in time to make you
forget you were mad? Angry Young Posers!
What does it take to embarrass you?
Do the Knights of Columbus have
to brandish their swords before
you sit down and watch the movie?

Meanwhile the Ravishing Latin Girls
are dressed up for Mardi Gras and
teaching each other spectacular dances.
Meanwhile the Glorious Irish Girls
have charmed a fin from each bagpiper,
and this keg of beer is magically replenished.
Meanwhile the Magnificent Italian Girls
have squeezed into one stretch limo
for the mother of all Bachelorette parties
Meanwhile the Fascinating Black Girls
are rapping like warrior poets,
and those who do not rhyme do listen closely.

(And under a hand-carved arch on Castle Hill Avenue,
Two homeless teenagers cradle their newborn son.)

44 Back in the Holy Bronx

Holy Bronx, you sway with righteous whimsy.
Holy Bronx, you call all choirs to perfect pitch.
Holy Bronx, you assume the proper posture,
and you wait for whatever happens next.
Lilt of the Holy Bronx upon my tongue;
Bounce of the Holy Bronx in my walk;
All the way up Webster Avenue from now
until Yonkers, Amen.

I am back in the Holy Bronx,
and I don't know about you, Monsignor, but
I still see the grandeur of the Grand Concourse.
I am back in the Holy Bronx,
and you Swells of Riverdale can just stop
pretending that you live in Westchester.
I am back in the Holy Bronx,
Wishing that I could drop everything
and venerate the Stonehenge
gazebo off Allerton Avenue, or
fathom the terracotta hieroglyphics
of Parkchester, or leer like Leif
Erikson as I leap off my dragon and
claim City Island for Odin.

Holy Bronx, you are what you are
as the names of illustrious Jews baffle
the denizens of Co-op City.
Holy Bronx, you are what you are
as Richard Wagner's Opera All-Stars
are strangely commemorated in Throgs Neck.
Holy Bronx, you are what you are
as thoroughfares named for great French
Generals run past your hospitals and cemeteries
Holy Bronx, you are what you are,
as the Virgin Mary shows up at the Grotto,
looking much younger than pictures suggest,
and teaches a few words of Aramaic
to black-clad little old ladies

Who were once Ravishing Latin Girls
looking out for one another and bringing
their pay envelopes home unopened.
And who were once Glorious Irish Girls
coming to the door in their grandmothers'
sweaters to say that they were grounded
And who were once Magnificent Italian Girls
loosing the very brothers they used to
smack around on the neighborhood bums.
And who were once Fascinating Black Girls,
utterly un-self-conscious, hopeful even
as the room filled up with empty promises.
And the power of Grace is precisely that
they are what they were, and will always be so.

Holy Bronx, you nod with all-knowing.
Holy Bronx, you laugh with rueful recognition.
Holy Bronx, you wish your Ponce De Leons well,
and leave their house keys in the mail box.
Lilt of the Holy Bronx upon my tongue;
Bounce of the Holy Bronx in my walk;
All the way up Webster Avenue from now
until Yonkers, Amen.

J.R. McCarthy is a high school teacher from the Bronx. He lives in an amazing apartment on the outskirts of Bronxville, NY, with his beautiful and virtuous wife, Tricia, and entirely too many books. He watches too much television, and he doesn't get enough exercise. He hates umbrellas and cream cheese. He doesn't care for suspense. He tries to be a good husband, a good son, a good brother, a good uncle, and a good friend. He tips like a drunken sailor. He is as young at this moment as he is ever going to be.

He started writing poetry almost immediately. He started trying to publish his poetry when he became tired of waiting around to be offered the role of Ignatius Reilly in the movie version of *A Confederacy of Dunces*. He is (no fooling) the lead singer of The Sleepers, the world's most dignified and self-possessed Rock and Roll band. He wrote a novel about shoplifting when he was 11 years old. It is entitled *Sticky Fingers*. No one may read it under any circumstances.

J.R. McCarthy acknowledges, and wishes to be acknowledged by, the saints and angels by whom he is completely surrounded. He sends his love and regards to his students past and present. He believes that T.S. Eliot was absolutely right when he said that humility is the only wisdom we can hope to acquire. The moment he read that, in *The Four Quartets*, he began to write *Ambivalid*. He announces with cautious optimism that *Ambivalid* is now finished. Let him know what you think.

Visit J.R. McCarthy at http://jayarespoems.blogspot.com/